When Life Hurts

Knowing God is with you

SELWYN HUGHES

CWR, Waverley Abbey House, Waverley Lane, Farnham, Surrey GU9 8EP, England.

NATIONAL DISTRIBUTORS

AUSTRALIA: CMC Australasia, PO Box 519, Belmont,Victoria 3216.
Tel: (052) 413 288

CANADA: CMC Distribution Ltd., PO Box 7000, Niagara on the Lake, Ontario
LOS 1JO. Tel: 1-800-325-1297

INDIA: Full Gospel Literature Stores, 254 Kilpauk Garden Road, Madras 600 010.
Tel: (44) 644 1353

KENYA: Christian Products Ltd., PO Box 56495, Nairobi.
Tel: (02) 567516

MALAYSIA: Salvation Book Centre (M), 23 Jalan SS2/64, Sea Park, 47300 Petaling
Jaya, Selangor. Tel: (3) 7766411

NEW ZEALAND: CMC New Zealand Ltd., PO Box 949, 205 King Street South,
Hastings. Tel: (6) 8784408

NIGERIA: FBFM, (Every Day with Jesus), Prince's Court, 37 Ahmed Onibudo
Street, PO Box 70952, Victoria Island. Tel: 01-2617721, 616832

REPUBLIC OF IRELAND: Scripture Union, 40 Talbot Street, Dublin 1.
Tel: (01) 8363764

SINGAPORE: Campus Crusade Asia Ltd., 315 Outram Road, 06–08 Tan Boon Liat
Building, Singapore 169074. Tel: (65) 222 3640

SOUTH AFRICA: Struik Christian Books (Pty Ltd), PO Box 193, Maitland 7405,
Cape Town. Tel: (021) 551 5900

USA: CMC Distribution, PO Box 644, Lewiston, New York 14092-0644.
Tel: 1-800-325-1297

When Life Hurts

Copyright © CWR 1997

Design and Typesetting: CWR Production

Printed in Great Britain by Clifford Frost

Photographs: Corel Corporation, Photodisc

ISBN 1 85345 112 6

Material originally published in EDWJ

Introduction

The theme for this special series brims over with hope and confidence – a hope and confidence that are so much needed in those times when we are called to walk in darkness.

The secret of *why* God chooses to lead us into the darkness is revealed to us in Isaiah 45:3 *"I will give you the treasures of darkness, riches stored in secret places, so that you may know that I am the Lord."* There are treasures which can only be found in the dark. John Bunyan found them in the darkness of a prison and wrote the immortal *Pilgrim's Progress*. Helen Keller, blind and deaf, found treasures in her darkness and shared them with the world through her glowing spirit. In a deep dark well you can look up and see the stars, even when people in the light above cannot see them. We can discover treasures in the darkness that we would never be able to find in the light.

When we find ourselves surrounded by darkness we must look for the meaning that lies within it. Many Christians allow the darkness to drag their spirits down to such a degree that they lose their faith. They do not know how to search out the treasures that lay all around them.

When Jesus took upon Himself our flesh He deliberately and voluntarily limited Himself to finding out about life in the way we find out – by grappling with issues day after day. He learned about the treasure that is in the darkness of suffering.

We are not going to be exempt from the difficult periods of life just because we are Christians. If we have this attitude it will hinder us from discovering the treasures that are all around. Periods of darkness can be times of great spiritual advance providing we stand up to them with the right attitude which says that God will allow nothing to come into my life unless it can be used.

The apostle Paul found grace in the darkness of a prison experience and when our souls are open to that grace which constantly flows towards us from heaven then every difficult situation can be the setting for a new discovery of God and a new revelation of His love.

If at this moment you find yourself in darkness and your heart is broken and dispirited, then give God all the broken pieces and allow Him to put your life together again, perhaps in a new and more glorious pattern.

In this booklet we look at three areas which cause us hurt in our lives: suffering and pain, bereavement and loneliness. Knowing God is with us during these times can bring the comfort and support which is so much needed. In times when there appears to be little hope and relief there are treasures to be found even in these periods of darkness.

Suffering and Pain

After
the avalanche

A form of darkness in which we sometimes find ourselves engulfed is that of suffering and pain. It is at this point that the faith of many experiences its deepest shocks. A woman

"In all this, Job did not sin by charging God with wrongdoing."
(v. 22)

writes: "My sister was a very godly woman but she suffered so dreadfully in childbirth. Why didn't God spare her this suffering since she was such a godly woman?" A professor in a great Christian university in the United States of America was hit by a truck, knocked down and suffered a broken leg. After he recovered, he told the students in the morning chapel: "I no longer believe in a personal God. If there were a personal God, would He not have whispered to me to beware of the danger of the oncoming truck and have saved me from this calamity?" The professor was struck and in the fall his faith crashed too.

For further thought

Psa. 84; Isa. 40:31, 41:10; Eph. 3:16

1. What is the reward of the upright?

2. Consider how the RV brings out the meaning of Psalm 84:6: "Passing through the valley of Weeping they make it a place of springs."

Can God hold us fast in such times? Can we find treasures in this darkness, too? With all my heart I say – we can. The ancient patriarch Job wrote more than patronising platitudes about suffering: he'd been there and back. He could describe intense suffering in the first person because of his own sea of pain. Blameless, upright, clean-living and respected by everyone – God included – he experienced a wave of calamity that almost blotted him out. He lost his livestock, crops, land, servants and every one of his ten children. Soon after that he lost his health, his last human hope of earning a living. How did he react to all this? Well, you read his response in the words of our text.

Right now I'm shaking my head with amazement as I consider his words. Would I have responded in such a way? Would you? I wonder.

A recipe for handling problems

Job 42:1–17

"I know that you can do all things ... Surely I spoke things I did not understand ..." (vv. 2–3)

We have looked at the darkness which engulfed God's servant Job and now we ask ourselves: how could he go through all that and not rail against the Almighty? Just think of it – bankruptcy, pain, ten fresh graves – yet we read that he worshipped God. He did not sin, nor did he blame his Maker. The question raises itself to almost cosmic proportions: why? Why could he ward off bitterness and still maintain his faith?

I think one reason was because Job looked *up* and accepted the fact of God's sovereignty. He sincerely believed that the Lord who gave had every right to take away. He had no arguments over God's rule in his life and believed that God's sovereignty was laced with love. Another reason was because he counted on the promise of resurrection: "I know that my Redeemer lives, and that in the end ... I will see God" (Job 19:25–26). He not only looked *up* – he looked *ahead*. He counted on God's promise to make all things clear at the Resurrection. He knew that at that time all pain, death and sorrow would be removed. Job endured the day to day happenings in the light of the next day's envisioning. A further reason was because he looked *within* and confessed his own lack of understanding. Our text puts this point most effectively. Job confessed his inability to put it all together and did not feel compelled to know just why God allowed things to happen to him in the way they did. God was the judge: that was fine with Job.

For further thought

Rev. 21; Psa. 30:5, 34:19;
Isa. 43:2

1. What is the hope of the believer?

2. What is the promise for the present?

That was how Job picked up the pieces after the avalanche had struck. It takes a firm faith to respond like that, but the fact that Job did it shows it can be done.

The inevitability of suffering

We continue meditating on the question of suffering and pain. It's surprising how many believe that God should spare good-living people from calamities and troubles.

Job 5:1–18

"Yet man is born to trouble as surely as sparks fly upward." (v. 7)

Suppose it could be guaranteed that calamities would always strike the wicked alone and that the righteous would always be saved – what kind of world would it be? Its laws would always be in a process of suspension to accommodate the righteous. Gravity wouldn't pull you over a parapet even though you leaned out too far – provided, of course, you were a Christian. The universe would no longer be dependable, for in any situation involving another person you would never be sure which laws would act for you. Much would depend on the character of that other person – and that would only be clear after the event had taken place – one way or the other! Such a situation would be ridiculous.

I do not question that God can and sometimes does intervene and save His children in particular situations, for one thing is sure – you cannot put God into a straitjacket in His own universe. The laws He has designed for the running of the universe are His habitual way of maintaining it, but He is perfectly capable of suspending those laws when He sees fit. Such an event we call a miracle. But miracles, by definition, cannot be the norm.

For further thought

Job 19; Psa. 27:1–14; Mal. 4:2

1. What was Job's affirmation despite his pain?

2. What was the Psalmist's declaration?

When Jesus hung upon the cross, the crowd cried: "He trusted in God; let Him deliver Him" (Matt. 27:43, NKJ). God did not deliver Him; *He did something better*. And it is along this line of the "something better" that we must search for the Christian solution to the problem of suffering.

God has suffered too

Isaiah 53:1–12

When all human attempts to relieve suffering and pain do not work and even prayer seems not to prevail – what then? Though there may be no

"Surely he took up our infirmities and carried our sorrows ..." (v.4)

miracle of deliverance, we must nevertheless believe that God is still at work and is with us in the suffering and pain. God did not rescue Christ from the sufferings of the cross because it was only through the sufferings of the cross that His perfect purposes could be achieved. This is the key – *God only allows what He can use*.

Christianity is the only religion in the world that dares to ask its followers to believe that God can work through suffering and pain, because it is the only religion that can say its God has suffered too. How much has God suffered? Some think He suffered only during the hours that Christ hung upon the cross, but there is much more to it than that. Christ was the "Lamb slain from the foundation of the world" (Rev. 13:8, NKJ). Can you see what that means? Ages before the cross was set up on Calvary there was a cross in the heart of God. The piercing pain of Calvary went through the heart of the Almighty the moment He laid the foundations of the world. Throughout the long millennia of history God carried with Him the pain of being parted from His only begotten Son. Then came the awful moment when it happened on Calvary. And was that the end of God's sufferings? No, now His sufferings continue in the world's rejection of His Son and at times in the indifference of some of His children – you and me.

For further thought

**Mark 14–15;
Heb. 4:15–16**

1. List 10 aspects of pain suffered by Christ.

2. How was He able to face it?

Doesn't it mean something, even everything, to know that though living in this world costs us suffering and pain, it costs God more? I find this thought deeply comforting. I pray that you will too.

A priceless treasure

Of all the letters Paul wrote, his second letter to the Corinthians is regarded as the most autobiographical. In it the great apostle lifts the curtain that hung over his private life and allows us to catch a glimpse of his human frailties and needs. You really need to read the whole letter in one sitting to catch the emotion that moves and surges through Paul's soul. It is in this letter that he records the specifics of his anguish, tears, afflictions, Satanic opposition, beatings, loneliness, imprisonment, hunger, shipwrecks, sleepless nights and so on. And what came out of it all? What were the treasures that were discovered in the darkness?

One treasure is found in the word "comfort". The word appears again and again in the passage before us. Because he had suffered, the apostle was able to enter into other people's problems with a capacity that he would never have had if he had not gone through those experiences. Have you noticed that when you have gone through a time of personal suffering and pain you are able to enter into other people's problems with more than a shallow pat on the back and a tired, "May the Lord bless you"? Now you have a genuine, in-depth understanding and sympathy. And you know exactly how to comfort others because you yourself have received the comfort of God.

2 Corinthians 1:1–11

"Praise be to ... the God of all comfort, who comforts us in all our troubles, so that we can comfort those in any trouble ..." (vv. 3–4)

For further thought

2 Cor. 3, 11:16–33, 4:7–10, 12:9

1. List 15 ways in which Paul was afflicted.

2. Where was Paul's sufficiency?

Are you suffering right now? Our loving heavenly Father is never preoccupied or removed when we are enduring sadness and affliction. He is there at your side this very moment. Let Him surround you with His special comfort and then, perhaps weeks or months later, you will be able to pass on that same powerful comfort to others.

Suffering and Pain

As you've read these pages I am sure that you must have asked the question, "is it really possible in the face of suffering and pain to respond like Job?". Do you long with all your heart to be able to respond to problems in your world like Job, with grace and not a grudge?

Today if you are in the midst of personal pain, take time now to talk with your Heavenly Father. Ask Him to help you to "look up and ahead" and, like Job, talk with Him about any lack of understanding that you may feel.

Consider also the suffering and pain experienced by God in giving His only Son and how He turned His pain to good account. Even though this issue of suffering and pain is one of the deeper mysteries of the universe – dare we believe that He does not deliver us because, as with Jesus, He has something better.

Ask the God of all comfort to help you not only receive His comfort, but to become a giver of comfort and that He would reveal this as one treasure from the darkness of suffering and pain.

Bereavement

Our most vulnerable moment

We look now at another form of darkness which at one time or another almost everyone has to face – the darkness of bereavement. In the very nature of things, hundreds of you reading these lines will be there right now. Others may have to face bereavement in the very near future, so we must learn how to enter this darkness with the confidence that there are treasures to be found even here.

Matthew 11:20–30

"Come to me, all you who are weary and burdened, and I will give you rest." (v. 28)

A fact that has always struck me whenever I have been with people who are in bereavement is that no matter how strong they may be at other times, whenever they are bereaved they become extremely vulnerable and thus open either to pain or consolation. J. Pierpoint Morgan, the American financier, was regarded as a tough and callous man; his biographer said that the strongest quailed before him. Yet when his wife died, he was so distraught that he cried out, "Won't someone please give me some comfort?" How human that is!

For further thought

Rom. 12, 15:1;
Acts 20:35; James 1:27; Gal. 6:2

1. How are we to respond to those who weep?

2. How can we be supportive?

Let's examine some of the "comforts" which the world offers to those who are bereaved. One is to drown one's sorrows in drink. Many faced with the loss of a loved one try to find refuge by soaking themselves in alcohol. Wanting to soften the pain inside them, they take what seems to be the easiest way to that end. But it is a failure. In the first place, it is horribly vulgar, and in the second, it is thoroughly ineffective. There is always the morning after, and the poignant memories return to haunt the mind – again and again and again. There is no true comfort in the "cup that cheers" – lasting comfort comes only through Christ.

Supplements are not solutions

We continue looking at the various kinds of comfort which the world offers to those who are bereaved, and now we look first at the comfort that comes from books. Some time ago someone showed me a statement made by a well-known "Agony Aunt" who has a regular column in a women's magazine. She was giving advice to someone who had been bereaved and this is what she wrote: "Find comfort in literature. The anodyne you need is good reading. Go along to your local library and get a good book. Lose yourself in it and you will find that it will do for you what it does for countless others – brings relief to your aching heart."

Isaiah 26:1–11

"You will keep in perfect peace him whose mind is steadfast, because he trusts in you." (v. 3)

For further thought

John 14; Rom. 8:11, 16; Gal. 4:6

1. What name does Christ give to the Holy Spirit?

2. How does He carry out this ministry?

I have no doubt that this advice is well-meaning but the worth of it can only be judged by those who love books. And not everyone does. People who have little interest in literature would find little help in this advice. A book can be a wonderful extra to those who need comfort, but it is absurd to expect a piece of literature to heal a wounded spirit.

Another way of the world is to recommend that one turn to nature. Lord Avebury, in his preface to his two volumes, *The Marvels of the Universe*, says: "Nature does much to soothe and comfort and console." I do not deny that there is a healing touch in nature. Multitudes who have been bereaved have gone out into the hills and felt ministered to by the power of nature, but once again, though it is a good supplement, nature is not a good substitute for the precious and powerful comfort that flows from Christ.

Art, nature, literature – all these may have a part to play in the life of those who are bereaved. They can help, but listen – listen – Jesus alone can heal.

Vita! Vita! Vita!

John 6:35–51

The central thought I now want to share with you is one that I wish I could write on the sky in letters of fire so that the whole world might see. It is this – *the Christian faith is the only faith that lights up that dark area of life which we call death*. And it lights it up, not with a word, but with the Word made flesh. Jesus went through death and thus the word of resurrection became flesh in Him. As it was said of Emerson: "He did not argue; he just let in the light," so it can be said of Jesus: He did not argue immortality; He simply showed Himself alive.

"... everyone who looks to the Son and believes in him shall have eternal life, and I will raise him up ..." (v. 40)

Many years ago, a missionary in Thailand was teaching a group of children about the cross and death of Jesus, and as the time had gone she was forced to end the story at the point where Jesus was laid in the grave. A little boy jumped into the aisle and said, "It's not fair – he was a good man." One little girl, who knew the full story, pulled him back to his seat and said: "Ssh! Don't make fuss – He didn't *stay* dead." Well, if He didn't stay dead, neither will we stay dead.

For further thought

2 Tim. 4:6–18; Rom. 14:8; Phil. 1:21; Psa. 23:4

1. How did Paul describe death?

2. How does the psalmist describe the presence of death?

A biographer says of Tennyson, "He laid his mind on the mind of others and they believed his beliefs." This is what our Lord does, only in an infinitely greater way – He lays His mind upon ours and we believe in His beliefs. And our Lord believed in and demonstrated immortality. No wonder the early Christians, shut up within the dark underground prisons, wrote on the walls: "Vita! Vita! Vita!" – "Life! Life! Life!" Prison walls could not quench or stifle this life, nor can death extinguish it. Can death stop a Christian? Stop him? It only frees him – for ever.

When diamonds look their best

Now that we have looked at some of the ineffective comforts that the world offers to those who are bereaved, and the sure confidence the Scripture gives us that in Christ death has been defeated, we are ready to ask ourselves: what are some of the treasures we can expect to find in the darkness of bereavement?

Deuteronomy 33:24–29

"The eternal God is your refuge, and underneath are the everlasting arms ..." (v. 27)

It is now several years since I laid my wife to rest, and I have been asking myself what treasures I discovered in the darkness of my own bereavement. One that immediately comes to mind is a new discovery of God and the truths contained in His Word. I had walked with the Lord for forty years before my wife was taken from me by cancer, and I had thought my intimacy with the Lord was about as good as it could ever be. I found, however, that the death of my wife produced in me a degree of grief and sorrow that I had never thought possible. I had known for several months that my wife's condition meant that her death was imminent but I was not prepared for the shock wave that went over me when it actually took place.

For further thought

Psa. 27:1–6, 31:19–21, 32:7, 119:14

1. What had the psalmist discovered?

2. What are you discovering?

The above verse is one that has always been a great favourite of mine, but now, since I have passed through the darkness of bereavement, it has taken on a dimension that is almost impossible for me to describe. Just as a precious diamond is best seen against a dark velvet background, so does the truth of God shine more beautifully when set against those black moments of life such as death and bereavement. The truth of God shines most beautifully at any time, but believe me, never more illustriously than when set against the darkness of a bitter and heart-rending experience.

— "a spiritual lifeline" if you like —

Grace that abounds

We have seen that one of the treasures we are likely to find in the darkness of bereavement is a new discovery of God and a new understanding of His Word. We may think we understand a truth of Scripture but we will never really understand it until that truth is the only thing we have left to hold on to. Deuteronomy 33:27 (the verse we looked at in the previous meditation) was always a favourite of mine, but now it is more than a favourite verse – it is a spiritual lifeline. I know its power in a way I never knew before because it held me in one of the darkest moments of my experience – bereavement.

Another treasure that we can find in this type of darkness is a more effective spiritual contribution to the life of the Church. Out of our personal sorrow comes a sensitivity and a concern for others that impacts their lives in a greater way than ever before. A couple of years after my wife died, a woman said to me: "I used to listen to you twenty years ago when you were a pastor in London, and although I was blessed by what you said, I always felt you were too demanding of us and a little hard. Now you are so different. The hardness has gone and a wonderful softness flows out of you." I tell you, a tear came to my eye as she talked because I recognised the truth of what she was saying. People tell me that in recent years there has been a new note in my writings, in my preaching, and in my teaching.

2 Corinthians 9:6–15

"And God is able to make all grace abound to you ... so that ... you will abound in every good work." (v. 8)

For further thought

2 Cor. 1; Matt. 5:4; Psa. 86:17

1. What was the psalmist's testimony?

2. Why are we comforted?

This is the treasure I found in my darkness.

If you are bereaved at this moment, or facing a possible bereavement, take heart – you will find treasures in the darkness that will remain with you for the rest of your life. He gives most when most is taken away.

Bereavement

Unfortunately there is just no way of escaping from the reality and darkness of bereavement. If this is something that you are facing, ask God to come alongside you today, drawing confidence from knowing that, with Him, you are able to face anything. Even though He cannot save you from it – He has promised to save you in it.

Consider for a moment all the "supplements" that have helped you. Thank God for them and for other people who support you, although these supplements will never be a substitute for our rock, the true and faithful God. Allow the Holy Spirit to help you fix your eyes upon the Author and Finisher of our faith.

Grief and sadness can be a backdrop and setting against which the truth of God and His comfort can shine more beautifully than ever. Whenever you feel engulfed, invite the Holy Spirit to help you expect a new discovery of Himself.

The need for consolation lies deep within our souls and is therefore inescapable – but ask God to enlarge your experience and help you understand that while He meets us in our grief, He longs to take us beyond it – to a greater understanding of Himself and a greater usefulness. Take comfort knowing that "the eternal God is your refuge, and underneath are the everlasting arms". (Deut. 33:27)

Loneliness

"Mankind's biggest problem"

Yet another form of darkness in which people sometimes find themselves is the darkness of loneliness. Can divine treasures be discovered there? With all my heart I say – they can.

Psalm 91:1–16

"I will say of the Lord, 'He is my refuge and my fortress, my God, in whom I trust.' " (v.2)

By "loneliness" I don't mean "aloneness". It must be understood at once that there is a great difference between loneliness and aloneness: it is possible to be alone and yet not lonely. The well-known psychiatrist and author, Dr Leonard Zunin, once said, "Loneliness is mankind's biggest problem and is the major reason behind the many and varied symptoms which I see in the people who present themselves before me day after day." So what is loneliness? It is the feeling we get when we are bereft of meaningful human companionship; it is a sense of isolation, of inner emptiness, deprivation and worthlessness.

For further thought

**Matt. 26:36–75;
Psa. 102:7; John 16:32**

1. How was Christ's loneliness increased?

2. Which lonely person can you befriend?

The poet Rupert Brooke records how, when he first set sail from Liverpool for New York, on May 22nd, 1913, he felt terribly lonely because no one had come to see him off. Everyone else had friends waving them goodbye – but not he. Looking down from the deck, he saw a scruffy little boy and swift as thought he ran down the gangway and said to him: "Will you wave to me if I give you sixpence?" "Why, yes," said the little boy. The sixpence changed hands and that day Rupert Brooke wrote in his diary, "I got my sixpenceworth in an enthusiastic farewell – dear, dear boy."

Those who have never felt the pangs of loneliness will find it hard to understand a story like that. But to others it will carry a world of meaning. It is a desolating experience to be lonely, yet the divine presence can so reveal itself that even this deep darkness is made bearable.

No one as lonely as He

We have said that there is a great difference between loneliness and aloneness. It is possible to be alone and yet not feel lonely. To feel lonely is quite terrifying. The feeling of

Matthew 26:36–56

"... Then all the disciples deserted him and fled." (v.56)

loneliness is not diminished in a crowd, or, for that matter, in a Christian church. Someone has described some churches – thankfully not all – as, "lonely places where lonely people go so that everyone can be lonely together". One can be *in* a crowd and not *of* it.

Did Jesus ever feel lonely? I cannot think that He would be able to sympathise with this problem had He not at some time in His life felt lonely. Since He was sinless, He would not have experienced the associated feelings of emptiness or worthlessness, but there were times when He was bereft of human companionship and in that dark hour on the cross He was bereft of divine companionship, too. The disciples were incapable of entering into our Lord's feelings as He agonised in the Garden of Gethsemane – how would He have felt about that, I wonder? On the eve of His death they argued about precedence; they slept while He wrestled in prayer; when He was arrested, they ran away. Most who have been willing to die for a cause have been able to comfort themselves that there were those who sympathised with them – but even this was denied Jesus. His self-sacrifice mystified the people who were His closest companions. Not one single soul understood why He allowed men to take Him and string Him up on a cross.

For further thought

Isa. 53, 50:6; Psa. 22:1;
Matt. 27:46; Psa. 37:25

1. What words of the psalmist did Christ echo?

2. What had the psalmist never seen?

However difficult it may be to face the darkness of loneliness, we know one thing at least – Jesus knows how it feels. Others may not be able to understand it, but our Lord most certainly does.

Solitariness – a trifle?

If, as we have been saying, there are treasures to be found in darkness, what is the treasure that can be discovered in the depths of loneliness? It may sound trite to some, but the answer is this – a deeper sense of the presence of God. An acquaintance of mine, a preacher who never married and who spends a great deal of time on his own, said this: "Loneliness, that precious opportunity for discovering more of God." He went on to say that he noticed that the times of his deepest loneliness were the times when Christ was most real to him.

Matthew 28:16–20

"... And surely I am with you always, to the very end of the age."
(v. 20)

F. W. Robertson, the prophetic preacher of Brighton, proved this. He was bitterly attacked by fellow Christians for his views, and as his brief life sped away his friends got fewer and fewer. It was in one of these dark periods, when it seemed that all his friends had gone, that he wrote: "I am alone, lonelier than ever, sympathised with by none, because I sympathise too much with all, but the All sympathises with me ... I turn from everything to Christ. I get glimpses into His mind, and I am sure that I love Him more and more. A sublime feeling of His presence comes about me at times which makes inward solitariness a trifle to talk about."

For further thought

Rev. 1; Acts 23:11;
Phil. 4:13

1. What was John's experience on Patmos?

2. How was Paul strengthened during his confinement in Jerusalem?

Look at that last sentence again: "A sublime feeling of His presence comes about me ... which makes inward solitariness a trifle to talk about." What a testimony! He found treasure in the darkness. With the assurance of Christ's presence vouchsafed to every Christian, there need not be utter loneliness in the hearts of God's children. Christ walked that way so that no one need ever walk it again.

Pause
– and consider

It would be impossible to discuss the subject of loneliness properly without making the point that some people bring loneliness upon themselves – they are lonely through their own fault. "Loneliness," says one writer, "is more of an attitude than a circumstance; more self-inflicted than outwardly caused. It is not just a matter of isolation, it is more a matter of insulation. Lonely people build walls

Romans 12:1–21

"Share with God's people who are in need. Practise hospitality."
(v.13)

around themselves and then complain of their loneliness." If we are in love with no one but ourselves, we can end up disliking everyone but ourselves.

Those who, like myself, find themselves in circumstances that compel them to live alone must watch that they do not become morose, critical, self-pitying and inward looking. These attitudes will reinforce even the slightest feelings of loneliness and quickly drive people away. "In a needy world like ours," said W. E. Sangster, "anybody can have friendship who will give it." And Emerson said many years ago: "The only way to have a friend is to be a friend." When anyone says, "I am friendless," he or she comes dangerously near to self-condemnation. The statement begs the rejoinder: "Have you *been* a friend?"

The Greek word *charis*, usually translated in the New Testament as "grace", also means "charm". God's grace can add charm even to the most morose personality. Have you noticed how two people in love sometimes become radiant? They not only demonstrate love to each other but it spills over to everyone else as well. Christ's presence in your heart will help you to be a friend, and being a friend means you will never have to concern yourself about having a friend.

For further thought

John 11:1–17;
Prov. 18:24, 27:10, 17

1. How did Jesus describe Lazarus?

2. Do something to foster a friendship today.

Where do you live?

We continue emphasising the point that there are treasures to be found in the deepest darkness – loneliness being no exception. We must be careful, however, that in looking for the treasures that lie in the darkness of loneliness, we don't make the mistake of pretending that loneliness is not a painful experience. There are some Christians who, whenever they sense that there is pain in an experience, pull away from it and pretend that it is not painful at all. That is an escape into unreality. Loneliness can be pretty painful and if it is, don't pretend that it is not. Christianity is not a religion of pretence; it is a religion of reality. We face the pain knowing that Christ can help us through it and turn the pain into something of benefit to Him, to others and to ourselves. The most important thing is to recognise that in all pain there are advantages. And the art is to admit the pain but focus on the advantages.

And what are the advantages of loneliness? What are the hidden treasures that lie within its darkness? The hurt or the pain brings deeper sensitivity to the problems of others, greater awareness of God's tenderness and nearness, increased self-understanding and the realisation that out of every pain God can produce a pearl. A visitor to an Old People's Home saw a man he knew, a Christian, and said to him: "I'm sorry to see you living in this Old People's Home." The old man drew

Acts 17:22–34

"For in him we live and move and have our being ..." (v.28)

For further thought

Psa. 42:1–11, 71:5; Jer. 17:7

1. What was the psalmist's predicament?

2. What was the psalmist's conclusion?

himself up to his full height and said: "My friend, I do not live in an Old People's Home – I live in God."

What about you, my lonely friend? Where do you live? All alone – or in God?

Loneliness

Consider for one moment, that whenever you feel alone, forsaken or forgotten – in truth you are not alone. The Holy Spirit is with you. Invite Him now to make this more than just theory; but to turn it to fact in your experience and life. Ask your Heavenly Father to sweep into your soul with an overwhelming consciousness of His presence.

Loneliness can be and often is terrifying. When the darkness of loneliness begins to raise its ugly head, pause to think about Jesus and how He also experienced loneliness and desertion by those He loved. Allow Him to draw near. Even though you may feel lonely, you need not feel desolate because He has promised to remain with you always.

Lastly, be open to change, invite the Holy Spirit to fill you with courage, to illuminate areas of opportunity for developing friendships knowing that He is not only with you, but *for* you also.

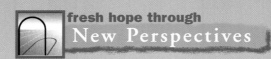

fresh hope through
New Perspectives

Difficult circumstances, particularly prolonged ones, can easily cause us to lose sight of God's perspective on our situation. New Perspectives aims to help people gain fresh strength and encouragement by seeing their circumstances in the light of God's Word and the grace He makes available. Thirty, easy to digest, daily readings gently unfold helpful Scriptures, practical insights and ideas for reflection and action.

A PLACE OF REST

Dr Bill & Frances Munro give practical advice on reducing stress.
1853451010

TODAY'S GRACE*

Frank Gamble shares an inspirational lifeline to all suffering from long-term illness. 1853451061

BREAKTHROUGH TO LOVE

David & Maureen Brown share valuable insights for building a better marriage.
1853451029

DOORWAY TO HOPE*

Helena Wilkinson offers fresh hope for those in despair. 1853451088

FINDING THE BALANCE*

Keith Tondeur provides practical advice on dealing with financial crisis.
185345107X

TOWARDS THE LIGHT

Dr Ruth Fowke offers experienced help for those going through depression.
1853451002

STRENGTH TO CARE

Hilary Vogel provides much-needed encouragement for carers. 1853451037

A WAY FORWARD*

Peter Curran gives encouraging help following redundancy.
1853451096

*Previously published under different titles.
96 pages   198 x 120 mm   Illustrated in colour   £4.95 each (UK)
Available from Christian bookshops or by post from National Distributors or CWR's UK distributors STL – Tel: 0345 413500 (local rate call).